FINE-TUNE YOUR CHOIR

Mike Brewer

© 2004 by Mike Brewer
First published in 2004 by Faber Music Ltd
3 Queen Square London WC1N 3AU
Design by Matthew Lee
Illustrations by Harry Venning
Printed in England by Caligraving Ltd
All rights reserved

0-571-52203-3

To buy Faber Music publications or to find out about the full range of titles available please contact your local music retailer or Faber Music sales enquiries:

Faber Music Limited, Burnt Mill,
Elizabeth Way, Harlow, CM20 2HX England
Tel: +44 (0)1279 82 89 82
Fax: +44 (0)1279 82 89 83
sales@fabermusic.com
fabermusic.com

Contents

This book is intended for the conductor with some experience of choral directing, for the chorister, or even the solo singer. In all these categories, it is assumed that the reader has an understanding of the general basics (as found in *Kick-start your choir*), and an awareness of the voice (*Mike Brewer's Warm-ups!*). Once the vocal engine is up and running, and a few miles have been covered, the concept of 'fine-tuning' comes into play.

By offering advice on intonation, rehearsing and performance skills, *Fine-tune your choir* will help to refine the sound of your choir and further explore the many facets of choral music – including singing in unfamiliar languages, reading skills, and particularly the thrill of creating a choral blend. It is not intended as an academic text, but offers an accessible introduction to the varied techniques involved in choral singing, and opens up opportunities for exploration in new areas. It is strongly advised that you also refer to the *Recommended further reading* section on page 47. But above all, have fun!

1 Preparation and rehearsal

You will find many books on choral conducting that deal well with score preparation and rehearsal technique (see *Recommended further reading*, page 47). However, here are a few tips to add to the basics:

❖ Be mentally inside the music before starting to conduct it.

❖ Look at every note and ask 'why'? For example: is it important or less important? Is it leading somewhere or static? Is it at a point of tension or relaxation? Is it light or dark? What colour is it? Is it long or short? Joined up or separate? Friendly or lonely? Youthful or mature? (Not to mention the old standby – happy/sad, angry/peaceful etc.)

❖ Explore every mark that the composer has made and ask yourself 'why'?

❖ Identify entries and main themes, and use colour markers or codes for them. Use other markers for dynamics, pauses and speeds.

❖ Make decisions on stylistic aspects (for example, the degree of lift of the crotchets/quarter notes, groupings of the quavers/eighth notes etc.) and be consistent.

❖ Like Mohamed Ali, keep dancing. Prepare and then react to what you hear.

Like Mohamed Ali, keep dancing

❖ Have an opinion on every aspect, but be ready to change it.

❖ Keep a dynamic relationship with the group so that they know to expect the unexpected. Remember that the brain settles into a routine, and needs to be reactivated.

❖ Always be positive in helping solve problems, and if you don't know the answer, see if someone else does. Don't bluff!

❖ Plan your rehearsal back from the end, and finish on a good moment.

❖ Never continue with something that is not going well (see *Kick-start your choir*).

❖ Find a comfortable pulse. Change the speed in different rehearsals, and don't go too fast.

- Don't settle on one performance early on.
- Never expect the next note.
- Incorporate sectional rehearsals, even with a choir with limited skills. Elect the best (or least worst!) in each group and let them lead the learning, then bring them back to show what they have done.
- Applaud every success, however small, but don't patronise or say something is very good when it isn't. Find something to praise and something to work on.
- Expect confidence from the singers. Applaud mistakes that you can hear! (The National Youth Choir has a prize for the best 'loud and wrong' note when sight-reading. 'Quiet and right' wins no prizes.)
- Aim high always. Go the extra mile (but not the extra minute!).

How to keep your rehearsal motoring

- Never sing a phrase in exactly the same way twice.
- Don't sing the next note yet; love the note you're with.
- In slow music, always feel the faster pulse.
- Don't use *vibrato* automatically, but to add colour.
- Always ask the lateral question.
- Lift and shorten weak word endings.
- For *legato* through words, lift the consonants and float the vowels.
- Remember that a *crescendo* is three dimensional, expanding all round the body, above the head, and into the floor. A *diminuendo* is equally three-dimensional. The sound should not become vapid as it lessens, but retain and focus its concentration.
- Renew the policy regarding vowels often (see page 16).
- Make descending scales more exciting by brightening the vowel as you descend.
- The vowel is always on the beat, so adjust consonant length accordingly before the beat.
- Remember that final chords are more effective without *vibrato*, unless they are high and loud.

Attention to basics is the quickest way to improve the quality of performance.

Posture

In a workshop situation, it is easy to transform posture instantly. Rather than waiting for this opportunity however, choral directors should ensure that their choir *never* sings a note without good posture. During a rehearsal, take a second to check posture before every new start. (See *Kick-start your choir* and *Mike Brewer's Warm-ups!* if a reminder is necessary.)

Breathing

Setting up good breathing can transform the sound instantly.

- Remember that the conductor's upbeat is a breathing beat, whether for instrumentalists or for singers.

- For all but very slow music, it is a good idea to give two upbeats to encourage slow breathing and give a sense of pulse.

Never sing a note without good posture

- Breathe in with the vowel shape of the first sung note, whether or not the piece begins with a consonant.

- End the music with lifted breath support, and offer it to the audience. (Don't use the hands, just feel the lift in the body.)

- There are many different schools of thought about breathing. If you are interested in the different 'schools' it would be worth more detailed study (see *Recommended further reading*, page 47). Advice to English singers: stick with simple and natural breath management (see *Mike Brewer's Warm-ups!*).

Trouble-shooting

A good sound-quality originates from listening and remembering.

To achieve or restore a desired quality of sound:

* ❖ If the sound is boring, flat or tired, check first for bad posture and have a signal for sitting or standing well. Simple postural signals (kinaesthetic and visual approaches, see page 9) save many minutes of talk and avoid the need to criticize verbally.
* ❖ Check the breathing.
* ❖ Check the vowels (see page 16).
* ❖ Check the onset of sounds and the clarity of the consonants.
* ❖ Check evenness of tone through the ranges, and good use of chest, head and mixed voice. (Consult a singing teacher as necessary. *Mike Brewer's Warm-ups!* also contains exercises to help.)

The art of learning and performing choral music is directly related to memory. Memory training should therefore be a high priority when preparing for your choir's next concert.

The 'five times' rule

The capability of the brain to recall information becomes faster with each repetition of the information, and seems to become instinctive only after approximately five repetitions. If rehearsals are weekly, it therefore makes sense to rehearse something five times over a term; each repetition separated by a night's sleep, at the very least. I have found the following formula to be true:

* ❖ The first time a phrase is sung, the 'thinking brain' reads it or the 'instinctive brain' hears it, and the singer can reproduce the phrase through a combination of reading and copying.
* ❖ The second time it is rehearsed, most of the information from the first time has been forgotten. It needs to be read, heard or seen again to jog the memory.
* ❖ The third time it can be reproduced more quickly and accurately, but the physical involvement in the sound-making still needs to be recalled. (See 'Kinaesthetic memory', page 9.)
* ❖ On the fourth repetition, the response is more physical and automatic, so the recall is faster still.
* ❖ The fifth time, with luck, the whole experience can be recalled quickly and automatically, i.e. the pitch, rhythm, words, sound colours, phrase and emotion.

During this process, all the different types of learning and memory (see below) are amalgamated to form the complete picture.

Types of memory

When employing the 'five times rule', the conductor should be aware that different choristers respond to different types of learning, so the activity should be varied as much as possible. Some singers read quickly, but instantly forget (many professionals!). Some can copy a phrase once heard, but can't read the music. Some remember photographically from the page. Some remember visually, and respond to the conductor's gestures. Some remember fact; others image. The different types of memory habitually employed are:

Factual memory: the absorbing of specific information. This incorporates awareness of patterns and structure as well as information from the page such as key, time and performance directions.

Kinaesthetic memory: training our muscles to memorize actions and repeat them. This is a very valuable tool for the conductor, because particular gestures can remind singers of the physical aspect of vocal sound-making and technique, bypassing conscious thought-processes. This is sometimes called 'right-brain' memory.

Visual memory: recalling a printed page or a visual experience. Remembering a phrase by seeing in the mind's eye how it looks on the page, or recalling a gesture of the conductor (linked to kinaesthetic memory).

Aural memory: remembering sounds. Often called 'inner hearing', which means the music can be 'heard' silently internally. Through training, this can be refined to greater degrees of precision, such as awareness of specific pitch, rhythm, harmony, hearing two parts at once, hearing chord sequences and cadences.

Just do what I do!

Mimicry: copying sounds and actions. This is the simplest kind of instant memory, very effective in teaching and learning, and not to be undervalued.

Emotional memory: recalling a mood, an experience, an expressive gesture or shape. This is vital in performance, setting the stage for a creative experience.

Mimicry is the simplest kind of instant memory

During the learning process the conductor should attempt to draw on each type of memory, thereby catering for individuals with different strengths and aptitudes.

Singing at sight

Sight-singing is simply the very fast recall of sounds. The techniques involved are therefore identical to those of memorizing, using the printed page as the source. It is best tackled through a practical and methodical approach, as can be found in the *Improve your sight-singing!* series.

Memorizing words

Since the verbal part of the brain is so much larger than the part devoted to musical sounds, it saves much time and effort to learn words separately, and then link them to the music. Try the following, varying the activity each time it is repeated:

* Read the words right through to discover the overall structure and meaning.
* Learn the first line and the last line straight away, to give an objective.
* Learn any line by straight repetition.
* Say the words of a line from memory with different rhythmic stresses, for example, accentuating the weak beats instead of strong. Accentuate all the unimportant words (like an airline announcer).
* Whisper the words.
* Say the vowels only.
* Say the words *staccato*.
* Say them in different regional accents.
* Say the words round the choir, one word or line at a time.

Memorizing music

As music is made up of patterns, it is more efficient to train ourselves to recognize these, rather than trying to work out each note individually. (Think how fluently we, as adults, read words and sentences – compared with our childhood attempts to work out each letter.) The skill of memorizing music can therefore be improved instantly.

* The most common error in sight-singing is not recognizing a repeated note. Try singing a phrase with your choir, and see if this is true.

❖ Another common error is not recognizing a note encountered earlier in the bar. Check if the pitch of a particular note is the same when it appears again, say, in an ascending and descending scale.

❖ Always sing in time, choosing as slow a pulse as needed. Enjoy the sensation of reaching the last note in time, and getting it right – whatever happens along the way.

❖ Think tonally, remembering the keynote both as a sound and as a position on the written stave (aural, factual, visual memory).

❖ Find the fifth of the scale and slot the brain into recognising it when it appears.

❖ Recognise scale passages in their key.

❖ Select the tonic chord notes from the scale. Be prepared for pitches 2 and 4 *not* being in the chord.

❖ Think in patterns, spotting repetitions – whether exact or altered.

Games to reinforce learning

❖ Sing only the first note of each bar/measure, counting silently and feeling the beats in between.

❖ Chose particular pitches and sing these pitches only, counting the rest of the music silently while listening with the inner ear.
(For example: in a piece in G major, sing only the Gs and Bs; sing only the first five notes of the scale where they appear in the music; sing everything except the fourth note of the scale, etc.)

❖ Let your choir be a human xylophone; each sing one note along the row. Stop and hold individual notes at random.

Let your choir be a human xylophone ...

❖ When conducting scales, use a gesture in contrary motion to the pitch direction; for example, in an ascending scale, gently press down with the non-beating hand. This will help with cross-lateral thinking and breath support. Ask the singers to make the same movements whilst singing.

4 | Blend

The team

The elusive blend that makes an outstanding ensemble is simple to achieve but rare to find. Blend should not be confused with a bland uniformity. Just as the colours of the spectrum combine to create an individual colour, a vibrant, blended choral sound can be created from a wide range of individual vocal colours.

Blend is created by asking all choristers to consider themselves contracted to the team (as in sport), and so to enjoy the same kind of training for the next match. As a team member, their individual strengths can be used to reinforce the whole team and the end product. It is important to remember that people sing in choirs to enjoy the companionship, the communal experience and the total sound. They enjoy it even more when challenged.

- ❖ Ask individuals to sing on their own in a rehearsal. Shy singers may object initially, but if you ask their help to illustrate a point, and ask lots of people in a row, it will work.

- ❖ Remember that a choir does not achieve real ensemble until every member feels valued.

- ❖ Quality of sound is not important, to start with: the priority is the positive contribution of each member.

- ❖ Get each singer to listen to each neighbour and check if he or she is making the same kind of sound at the same dynamic level. (Don't tell Fred he is too loud; invite him to encourage and blend with his less confident neighbour.)

A choir does not achieve real ensemble until every member feels valued

Blending individual people

The tackling of vowel sounds (see page 16) can effect a quick improvement, and therefore, addressing the choir as a whole is usually sufficient. However, in most choirs there are individuals whose sound actually works against the blend, and it is important to find positive strategies to involve them rather than criticizing them. A singer is two things at once: an instrument and a player, and individual singers are blessed in each category to different degrees. This difference is present at every level of choral singing.

Over a period of time, listen to every voice, ideally singing a short phrase alone, or as part of a small group. Classify each voice as: Dark/bright, rounded/square, wide/narrow, dull/strident, clear/breathy, straight/vibrated, strong/weak, or any classification of your own to differentiate their basic sound. Now compare the sound they make with their facial position.

Trouble-shooting blend

- Most tense sounds are accompanied by muscular tension and shallow breath support. A first step is therefore to focus on relaxation and breathing games.

- A 'square' and rather unblended sound is usually caused by a tense jaw, occasionally coupled with an exaggerated facial shaping, and the tongue may be held far back. At its extreme this combination causes a very strident sound. Remedy: ask the singer to relax the jaw in a natural way (See *Kick-start your choir* and *Mike Brewer's Warm-ups!*), and put the front of the tongue behind the lower teeth.

- An over-relaxed jaw, loose tongue and unfocussed face tends to produce a dull sound. Remedy: switch on the eyes! Combine the relaxed jaw with bright vowel sounds and an active tongue.

- A breathy sound is caused by air escaping through the larynx. To make the sound clearer, the singer can practise onset games (short animal noises/quick vowel sounds; see *Kick-start your choir*). This will take time to improve, but the whole choir can benefit.

- A dark, over-round sound is often made by lips held forward, sometimes rigidly, and the singer tends to enjoy that sensation. In fact, this sound is less likely to carry and will often be lost in a section. The singer needs to be convinced that jaw and lip relaxation actually makes for more resonance, coupled with the sub-glottal pressure that comes from good air support.

Solo singers, resonance and *vibrato*

'Solo singers will spoil their technique by singing in choir' is a generalisation that contains an element of truth. However, the real question is whether the solo singer has sufficient command of technique to harness it and use the positive elements that assist with blend and control.

Recent research (see *Recommended further reading*, page 47) demonstrates that the actual techniques used by singers in a choir are basically the same as in solo singing. Control is therefore the vital element. A soloist can make use of breath control, a 'floated' sound and half-voice in quiet passages, and can sing quite strongly in louder sections – rather than restricting the voice. Control of sound colour (varying a vowel or modifying *vibrato* where required) is equally valuable.

Vibrato is essentially a matter of style, and in much music its use to decorate dotted notes, for example, can be thrilling. Control is the important ingredient. Choral singers can learn how to use *vibrato* as a positive colour in sound rather than an unplanned presence (or absence). A really powerful voice may be simply too big to blend effectively. However, it is often the case

It is possible to take the positioning of individual singers to extremes

that an experienced solo voice under the control of its operator can blend superbly, and reinforce and provide a rich centre for the sound of a section.

Blending by placement

It is possible to take the positioning of individual singers to extremes so common sense is a crucial element, since individuals vary according to time of day, mood and concentration level. Much can be achieved simply by the positive commitment of the singers. However, some rules of thumb can be helpful:

1. Place opposite singer types (see page 13) next to each other, and encourage them to listen to their neighbour.

2. In groups of 2 or 3, ask the rest of the choir to listen as individuals change their vowel shape to match a neighbour.

3. Focus on the elements of the voice that blend most naturally: high resonance in the back of the neck, and vowel colours.

4. Help singers with particularly individual vowel sounds to modify them.

Sample standing plan

(To be modified for the concert according to singers' heights, of course):

❖ Centre row: a strong solo voice (not necessarily quick in accuracy) and a good reader/blender

❖ Next left and right of centre: a breathy voice, compensated for by –

❖ The next strongest solo voice, which helps –

❖ A bright or even strident voice, compensated for by –

❖ A dark, or rounded voice

❖ A clear, gentle voice

❖ Another breathy voice (there are always several)

❖ Another clear and accurate voice

❖ Another shy voice

Continue in this vein, depending on the numbers in each section. Every choir will have different ratios of these voices, but the general types above will usually be found.

Blending through vowels

Vowels are the carriers of sound, formed by the harmonics of a basic vocal sound. Every language and every region has its own repertoire of vowels, but the physical ingredients are always the same. Since we all pronounce words differently, using words as the basis of a choral sound is creating a hostage to fortune. However, once a choir agrees on a particular sound for each vowel, it can then be used as a resource for blending in any language or dialect. A blended sound within a group depends on each singer modifying his or her natural sound towards an agreed timbre and colour for every vowel. The actual sound suited to different repertoire and periods depends on personal ideas of style, but the most important factor is the conductor's awareness of the sound, and desire to refine it.

Bear in mind that every singer hears his or her sound internally first, via bones directly from voice to ear, and the sound is brighter internally than what is transmitted to the outside world. Adjustment is therefore important. With the exception of sopranos, all voices can usefully sing with a brighter sound than feels natural.

You may not need to use these descriptions, but it is helpful to know that singers tend to call the vowels æ ('uh'), a (as in 'bag'), ɔ ('o') and ɑ ('ah') 'open', because the tongue is down. The tongue back and lips forward u ('oo') and the tongue forward i ('ee') vowels are 'closed', because the tongue is lifted and the air passage through the mouth is narrower. In general we can say that closed vowels resonate strongly, and that open vowels are neutral and tend to need more air support. (For example, a wide lower back plus the feeling of a hard palate focus for ɑ ('ah') works wonders.)

Trouble-shooting vowels

❖ Vowel sounds can be remembered aurally and kinaesthetically – by repeated listening and sound-making until the muscles involved respond instinctively.

❖ It is wrong to suggest that there is one correct way to sing a vowel or to combine it with consonants. This depends on the style, language, historical period and the local flavour, mixed according to taste.

❖ When asked to copy a sung vowel, individuals will often sing something very different without realising, because of inner hearing of the sound (see page 9).

Just the sounds...

Make monkey sounds

❖ Some individuals need to be asked to sing a quite different (perceived) vowel to blend with a neighbour. This can be an exciting moment for the whole section. Many males sing vowels at least one shade darker than they realise. Just sing a vowel one step brighter. (See also 'Blending chords', page 18.)

❖ Blend a flat, English a ('ah') by asking the singer to change towards the vowel ɔ ('o' as in 'orange') and open the lips slightly.

❖ Blend a dark ɑ ('ah') by focusing the sound on the hard palate and opening the top lip slightly.

❖ Put your thumb on the roof of your mouth, behind the top teeth. Say ɑ ('ah'), then sing it on one note, into your thumb.

❖ Now place thumbs one each side of your face, nail upwards. Imagine the sound balanced on the thumb nails.

❖ Repeat the sound to a glide, slowly lifting your thumbs forward and upward with strong arms. Can you feel the firmness of the sound? Can you hear the resonance? Repeat without the thumbs, and aim for an even more focused sound.

❖ With the short vowel ɔ ('o' as in 'orange') in particular, many singers automatically sing o ('oh', for example the Latin 'dona' becomes 'donar' rather than 'donna'), while others will be nearer to ɑ ('ah'). The National Youth Choir of Great Britain rule covering most instances is: All o's are ɔ (as in 'orange'). (German is a striking exception however – see page 35.)

❖ With o ('oh'), beware the diphthong and take care that the sound does not become flat in tone and pitch. A really good o or, better still, ō (English 'aw') feels as if it is in the cheeks, just above the top teeth.

❖ ɛ ('e' as in 'egg') is a persistent cause of concern in English choirs. Only a full-blooded Yorkshireman can really say that open sound. 'Egg' is reasonable, but try 'kyrie'. We tend to resort to the longer vowel e ('air'), which can then migrate to what Americans call the 'schwa' – ə ('uh').

❖ Tongue-forward i ('ee') is hard for many English people, and is a staple element in Italian singing. Make monkey sounds on i ('ee') and reproduce the sound in the word you are working on. The sound needs to be high and bright to avoid a pitch drop and an emotional low.

❖ At the other extreme, tongue back u ('oo') is the least resonant and most pure sound in terms of harmonics, providing the most intimate *pianissimo* at lower voice pitches. The purest u ('oo') is not in the English language (though it is very much there in Welsh). It can be reached by blowing air through forward lips. Feel the sound in the top lip. At higher pitches it needs to be opened up a little (see 'Blending chords', below).

❖ A falsely 'posh' sound doesn't sound natural in the 21st century, so to compromise, lower voices should brighten the sound towards ō (English 'aw').

Vowels as harmonics

All sounds are made up of harmonics, audible in everything from telephone wires to bells, and every musical instrument. The voice is no exception, and every sound we emit contains a variable mix of high and low harmonics, producing timbres we can describe as harsh, gentle, dark, bright, warm, dull and so on. This is because a sound wave can be divided into halves, thirds, quarters and so on to infinity. (Think of a violin string, stopped in the middle with each half vibrating.) The half-length waves sound an octave higher than the fundamental note, quarter-length waves are two octaves higher, and the other lengths form pitches that we recognise in scales.

Different vowels at different pitches contain varying numbers of harmonics. When the harmonics are clustered together, their sound produces an audible pitch called a 'formant'.

Around 2800-3000 cycles per second there is a particularly strong cluster, called the 'singer's formant', which produces the resonance that enables opera soloists to be heard above a full orchestra. A vibrant choral sound makes use of this same formant, which is achieved through controlled air pressure from lungs to larynx (good support), tilted larynx, and a feeling of resonance in the back of the neck and head. The combination of formants and vowels is complex, so it is easiest to approach resonance through practical activities.

Blending chords

The most common cause of an unblended sound is an emphasis on the top part. In Christian church music from the Middle Ages onwards, the melody is often to be found in the tenor voice, which sang the monks' original chant. Other parts would be composed for countertenor, alto and soprano. Secular music used instruments that played chords, accompanying a solo melody. Choral music combines both roles – *counterpoint* where each vocal entry needs equal emphasis, and *harmony* where blend requires balanced tone and dynamics.

Choral basses the world over sing with a dark colour to the tone; pleasing and macho to the singer, but without the higher harmonics to carry to the back of a hall. Add to that a forced tenor, a vibrato-full alto and a piercing treble, and the parody of the amateur choir is there before us. The solution is simple, but the conductor's guiles are needed to convince the singers of this fact. Once a blended chord is achieved however, the choristers will hear and be convinced of the difference.

How to build a blended chord

It may be surprising to learn that, in a major chord, the major third is lower than it would be on the equally-tempered piano. The perfect fifth is slightly higher.

If the bass sings with a reasonably bright sound (vowel ɔ 'o' to ɑ 'a'), the sound will contain the lower harmonics making the notes of the fifth, octave and major third above, and the other singers will resonate with it. If the tenor is on the fifth of the chord, the sound should also be bright. If at the octave, the sound should be duller than the bass. If on a high third then a round sound will work best. Altos an octave above the bass need to sound less bright than the bass, not the other way round. A major third should be rich and round and a fifth, bright. Sopranos need to make a vowel sound at least one vowel rounder or darker than the bass.

To make the highest notes sound more pleasant we can modify the vowel and reduce the number of harmonics, without the audience noticing. The term 'covered sound' has long been in use by British singers, and refers to this process. Modified vowel sounds are much found in German, for example. As with all things, if we use this technique with discretion we can improve the blend of the choir instantly. Note that this applies particularly to long chords and to final chords in a piece. When music is moving rapidly, such detail is more difficult to achieve, and has less obvious effect.

In minor chords, because the minor third from the root of a chord is so high in the harmonic series (no.19), it is not an easy pitch to sing in tune or to blend (which is why the 'tierce de Picardie' is so often used for final chords, resolving on to the more comfortable major chord). A combination of low pitch and bright sound make it most convincing.

Note that the minor third between harmonics 5 and 6 (notes 3 to 5 in the major scale, or mi-soh) is very easy to blend. It is a basic component of much folk music from every country and lives on in pop music. Look for it in the music you are studying – it makes a good anchor.

Specific vowel combinations for blended chords

❖ The variation in alto and tenor vowels according to the pitch is the third, fifth or octave, as above.

❖ From soprano E upwards, the timbre can be dampened usefully by darkening the vowel in order to blend with other voices. (This does not apply to the same degree in solo singing, but is still worth trying to limit harshness of tone.) At the same time the jaw should naturally relax towards the ə ('uh') sound.

❖ Many sopranos will tighten the jaw and bring the tongue back for high sounds. This can be counterproductive, and give rise to a tight and rather strained sound. Aim to feel centred with wide, lifted ribs. Use back and waist muscles, and double check the relaxation of jaw, tongue, neck, shoulders, knees, ankles and feet.

Intonation

The main causes of flat singing are bad posture, breath support, vowel placement and, of course, not listening. Some basics of good intonation are outlined in *Kick-start your choir*. For most people though, achieving positive intonation is not a conscious thought process: it is a sensation. Many a choir rehearsal is spoiled because the conductor tells the hapless choristers that their intonation is wrong, and they must get it right. This activates the thinking brain, which tries to correct the error, is totally self-conscious, and takes away the focus from the expressive part of the brain. The remedy is to feel the magic when sounds behave musically in melody and harmony, and to rid ourselves of the mistake culture. Here follow some specific ideas to help with common pitch-loss situations.

Scales

Most lapses in pitch can be rectified by clear listening, using points of reference. Inexperienced singers (and players) singing a scale do so ritualistically, hoping to arrive at the end in roughly the right place. Simply listening to and monitoring each note works instant wonders with the pitch. Every healthy action in singing is based on creating a muscular balance – so by lifting something we can counteract gravity, which pulls pitch downwards. Ensure that you choir stands flexibly but strongly, raises the breathing apparatus and lifts their voices – not forgetting to relax the jaw and shoulders.

When we look at scales in more detail, of course the whole process is much more subtle. In an ascending scale, the second note on the piano is lower than the harmonic which the natural scale would choose (harmonic 9). Because we are conditioned to the sound of the keyboard however, we are liable to sing the note at keyboard pitch. If we think of the second of the scale as a bright note, we will find the natural pitch of it. In a major chord, the third is actually a low note, but in a scale the sound needs to be bright. The fourth, having no accessible harmonic, is a guess for us, and therefore hard for young children to learn. The fifth (harmonic 3) is bright, and should be the point to aim for when singing a scale. Again, the sixth is not an easily accessible note for singers (to European ears, it sounds sharp when played on a gamelan instrument), so we guess. The raised leading note (harmonic 15) is naturally high, leaving a very small semitone to the octave, which is something conductors and performers rightly aim for. In short, a good way to keep the intonation clear is *not* to try to raise the pitch of all the notes going up, but to anchor the fifth and the octave in the mind.

In descending scales the same applies exactly. Sing the scale very slowly at first, anchoring no. 5 on the way, and checking back. Because 3 is comfortable (not high), 2 then needs to be bright, with a big step back down to 1. This combination of melodic and harmonic thinking is as difficult for the choral conductor as for the instrumentalist. Remember that in slowly changing chords, the harmonic blend is paramount, but in fast-moving melody the direction of the tune takes precedence.

Tuning within sections

Here the same procedure works as with vowel matching (see page 16). Listen down the line, and identify who is exercising the democratic right to sing at an

Listen down the line and identify who is exercising
the democratic right to sing at an individual pitch

individual pitch. A vowel that is flat in pitch will result from over-closing of the lips, tongue and throat, as well as from lack of breath-support. Replacing it with a more open vowel will instantly focus the sound and help it blend in the section. Sometimes we need to ask just one or two people to make the change (see 'Blending individual people', page 12).

Trouble-shooting

Singers who have more serious difficulty with pitching are actually deficient in pitch memory. The secret is regular repetition, to train the aural memory, and when sung, the muscular memory. (Having placed a singing hamster toy on his desk, the author can now anticipate the pitch of the first note, simply by constant repetition over a matter of days.) 'Tone deaf' people can generally improve substantially over a period of time by repeating simple pitches and pitch changes. If a singer cannot match your pitch, always start with his or her pitch. As soon as the singer recognises a change in pitch and can reproduce it, you are on the road to learning. If response is poor, try sirens (see *Mike Brewer's Warm-ups!*). Sometimes the vocal apparatus needs to be awoken to the possibility of pitch change. Step by step, you can then introduce the singer to the concept of 'up and down' in pitch, and then to specific pitches – exactly as a baby learns.

At the other extreme, some professional singers of Renaissance and of the most complex of avant-garde music differentiate pitches to an astonishing extent. Somewhere between the two extremes come most of us; happy with a comfortable blend and unhappy with what sounds 'out of tune'.

Singers with 'absolute pitch' memory are faced with interesting challenges in the choral context. If any members of your choir are blessed with that facility, a compromise deal can be effective. Ask them to agree:

1. To help the choir by giving pitches vocally, thus avoiding the need for the percussive piano note so beloved of choral conductors. How about using the first vowel of the piece? If you don't have such a chorister, please think of using a melodic instrument for pitch-giving.

2. To be tolerant of the pitch differences that happen inevitably in rehearsal, and to point out when the variance is excessive.

6 Flexibility

Real music rarely consists of pure *legato*, endless *staccato* or constant dynamics. The secret lies in finding an appropriate combination of techniques to create the musical effect required. It is therefore important to know what we want to achieve with any musical phrase. Remember, in a rehearsal, don't say what you want: show what you want!

Legato

A common failure of understanding among singers is what *legato* actually is. A simple way to develop awareness is to think of instrumental techniques:

❖ Sing a simple scale slowly to a vowel.

❖ Listen to the sound and see how much it changes during each note, and from note to note.

In real *legato* you cannot hear the join between the notes. Air flows smoothly so the larynx is not 'pushed' on each note. Support muscles should be fully engaged, vowels merge effortlessly, and resonant consonants keep the sound alive. Lip and tongue consonants flick quickly and clearly, causing minimal disturbance to the flow.

❖ Ask the choir to sing a slow glide to join up notes of different pitches. This will keep the vocal apparatus energised, and the sound even.

❖ Repeat, speeding up the glide.

❖ Use conducting gestures to reinforce the choir's visual memory for *legato*. Vertical movements tend to collapse the breathing and work against you, while horizontal movements are magically effective in maintaining tone.

❖ Use images, for example: a violin bow moving evenly over the string, with wrist movement at the bow change. (Try at different speeds and with different imaginary weight applied with the bow arm.) Ironing a long item like a sheet or trousers; spreading butter over a long loaf of bread; flattening sand in a large tray. (Arm weight links directly to the muscles of support when breathing, and evens and deepens the sound.)

Staccato

Staccato is *legato* with gaps. The danger is that singers energise each note too slowly for it to work when the notes are very short. Remedy: basic 'onset' games (see *Kick-start your choir* and *Mike Brewer's Warm-ups!*). Sing the *staccato* phrase *legato* first. Then change it to a dotted rhythm, or two short and two long notes. Remember, when using technique games, vary the activity with each repetition.

Rhythm

Most of the human race feels and dances a rhythmic pulse. Choral singers generally count it. Kinaesthetic, muscular learning is twice as effective as just thinking so to establish a pulse in the mind, ground it in the body first.

❖ In very slow music, provide a constant quaver/eighth note accompaniment by tapping on a drum or radiator, or asking the singers to articulate the rhythm in repeated quavers/eighth notes while singing. Try articulating the vowel again on every quaver/eighth note.

❖ Subdivide complex rhythms, if they become slack—sing all three quavers/eighth notes of a dotted crotchet/quarter note, for example. In syncopated rhythms, ask half the choir to give a pulse beat (not clapped, because that will speed up). Try a gentle tap with feet, or hand on thigh, to ground the pulse.

❖ Remember the dance; think of lifting from the feet through the whole body.

At least its just bubonic, and not the ubiquitous *mf* plague!

Avoid the ubiquitous *mf* plague

Dynamics

In any choir, dynamics range between the enthusiastic *forte* of some adult groups to the tentative sweetness of some children's choirs. In order to avoid the ubiquitous *mf* plague, don't tell the singers the dynamics you want; instead, offer them choices. Either look in the score for helpful information or watch the conductor for the same reason!

The following are some games to develop dynamic awareness and subtlety:

❖ Sing a chord at a loud dynamic. Now repeat it many times *staccato*, re-energising every time. Now repeat getting quieter, but taking at least 8 repeats before reaching a quiet dynamic. Repeat at different speeds to different vowels.

❖ Draw a line on a board, select Italian dynamic terms and place them along the line in sequence from softest to loudest. Ask the choir to sing as someone points to dynamics along the line.

❖ Now point to dynamics between the known points and sing those.

❖ Now sing *crescendo* and *diminuendo*, using points of reference along the line. Keep the sound even between the dynamics. Repeat with different vowels. Repeat, changing the vowel as the dynamic changes.

❖ Think of dynamics as a wide series of options, based on character of sound and expressive needs. Try asking the choir for a warm glowing *mf*, a rich *f* with the sound going sideways instead of forward, an intense *pianissimo* etc.

Without thinking, we tend to push the sound through the larynx harder (shout!) for loud sounds, and whisper for soft. However, although useful for dramatic moments, they are both harmful to the voice when used unthinkingly. Therefore, we need to acquire the skills of gradually enriching and lightening the tone by singing on the breath instead. This is the basis of what is commonly called 'Mesa di Voce', which combines different kinds of voice production in an even way.

Velocity, coloratura

Remember that a short note requires the same basic technique as a long one, so start by ensuring that the sound is grounded in good onset, good support and good lift. The rest follows.

❖ For very fast runs on a vowel, try a slight aspiration. Think of the whole run as one long note separated, rather than a series of short ones.

❖ If the tempo allows, use a gentle onset on every note. Think of 'renewing' the note every time. (Animal calls and warm-up games will help here.)

❖ With consonants, practise lips and tip-of-tongue games. Check that you are not using the whole apparatus of the tongue back and the jaw, and that the throat stays open.

❖ Practise tongue twisters, and make them up to fit the difficult phrase.

❖ Subdivide the whole passage into phrases, noting the repetitions, sequences and changes.

❖ Check where the stresses are, as they may be unexpected. Look for where the new phrase starts and renew your energy there.

❖ Use dynamics to keep the energy alive (for example, in Handel anthems).

❖ Remember to darken the colour of the vowel on higher notes; sopranos in particular.

7 Style

When preparing any piece of music, the conductor needs to ask a range of stylistic questions. There are no right or wrong answers (though it is vital to steer clear of cultural relativism and of performing music without understanding its place in the life of its country), but it is important to be aware of stylistic elements in the music of different periods. What makes a performance exciting may not be the actual style in which it is sung, but the fact that the conductor is demonstrating stylistic ideas. We may disagree with the conductor's interpretation, but we are being given something to bite on.

When trying to sing a piece in a particular style, we often find ourselves adding something or attempting to adapt what we already do. (Be warned that it is dangerous to attempt to imitate musical styles that are impossible without years of exposure to their culture and techniques; for example the throat harmonics of Tuva, or the polyrhythms of Cuba.) However, it is more useful to look at some of the ingredients of different styles and try to work from the ground up instead. The following is very much a shorthand method for achieving an interesting flavour in performance, and does

The fool! I told him not to imitate the polyrhythms of Cuba!

It is dangerous to imitate musical styles without years of exposure to their culture

not replace a scholarly approach to good practice. The *Recommended further reading*, page 47, should serve as a useful starting point for exploring the stylistic elements of historical periods in greater depth.

Song and dance

If we remember that all music is made up of song and dance, then we can take a radical look at our intended repertoire. The Baroque suite was made up of a series of dances from all over Europe and from Africa too. It is a thrill to realise that the Chaconne of Bach comes from West Africa and that many themes from the symphonies of Mozart are those of Turkish folksongs. Renaissance music for the church, which has formed the basis of our choral repertoire for centuries, derives not only from plainsong but also from those same mediaeval dances that inform our secular music.

Renaissance music

❖ The musical phrase originates from words and dance, so combine the gentle stress of the words with a lift of the toes. Keep the feeling away from your heels!

❖ Remember the Trinity. Christian music of this period is devoted to the concept of 3 as the perfect number. Think in threes!

❖ Triple metre dominates verbal phrasing. Enjoy articulating it.

❖ It is rewarding to look at any piece of Renaissance church music, mark the verbal stresses and see how many three-beat shapes the verbal phrases make. Simply singing those stresses in a natural way brings complex counterpoint to life. (Even more fun can be had looking for fives, especially in Byrd.)

❖ This process applies to the music of every country, even in the apparently academic pieces of Palestrina for example, and stunningly in the music of Byrd and the English school. It works just as well with Victoria, Schütz and all the Renaissance masters.

❖ Find a natural pulse and keep every section of longer works in proportion to it. Particularly in the Psalms of Schütz, for example, there can be four different speeds from semibreve/whole note to quaver/eighth note, but maintaining an underlying minim/half note (= dotted minim/half note in some sections) pulse throughout. (Psalm 84 works sublimely in this way, for example.)

❖ Use a sensible alternation between dance rhythms and seamless *legato*, and sometimes both at once in different voices.

❖ Use the emotion of the story to dramatise the music. Most composers do not offer you the emotion on a plate though – you need to identify and inflect it. (Victoria's *Dixit Dominus*, for example, is written in clear and even counterpoint, even in the most harrowing moments. The conductor can thus use the dance rhythms, hidden threes and dramatic words to bring an extra dimension to a performance, while maintaining the iconic evenness of the basic style.)

- In counterpoint we need to hear the subject entries clearly, so avoid clogging the texture with less important voices.

- If crotchets/quarter notes (or minims/half notes in old notation) are repeated, lift them with the toes, as above.

- If in a scale, phrase them in a way which focuses on the verbal stresses, either short or long according to your feeling of the mood.

- Do not let your crotchets/quarter notes either dominate, or be boring. Stroke them kindly. Do not stamp on them.

- Support your quavers/eighth notes (or crotchets/quarter notes in old notation). They are used to make patterns decorating the cake. Identify the patterns and find a phrasing that feels good. As with crotchets/quarter notes, don't make them either too important or too boring. Vary short and long according to the mood and the moment. Enjoy appoggiaturas.

- Dotted crotchets/quarter notes are where music can come to life in the dance. Treat each one as a tennis ball; lob it gently into the air, and then strike it with gentle accuracy on the quaver/eighth note that always follows. This brings a hemiola (or, for pedants, a sesquialtera) to life.

- In harmonic sections, look for the drama. In renaissance music there is always a reason for chordal moments. They can be affirmative, jubilant, reflective or despairing.

- Since Renaissance church music does not clash, the prime source of intensity is the suspension. The extent to which you milk the opportunity is a matter of taste, but whatever you do, don't miss it!

- Latin pronunciation varies depending on the country where a piece was composed. (See 'Latin', page 42.)

- Spot the word painting, particularly in madrigals. Look for sudden harmonic changes, changes from solo to chordal sections, pairings of voices, or sudden very long or short notes.

Baroque music

Much of the Renaissance style is carried forward into Baroque music. Since most is accompanied by an orchestra, it is important that the choral role is identified in the overall texture. Handel is influenced by opera, and in his music and that of contemporaries in Germany, Italy and France, chordal sections alternate with instrumental-style counterpoint. To perform Bach it is helpful to identify three elements: the protestant hymn, or chorale; academic instrumental counterpoint, specifically the fugue; and dance.

- ❖ 'Baroque' means 'decorated', so enjoy the cornices and the pediments, the fireplaces and the foppery. Don't let the quavers/eighth notes get pedantic; remember they are only the icing on the structural cake.

- ❖ Patterns are all. Identify the sequences, the imitations, the echoes, and have fun shaping them. Surprise the audience with dynamic contrasts in repeated phrases.

- ❖ Remember the gestures of baroque dance. Musical phrases are full of bowing curtseying, glove waving, greeting and farewell. Always keep on your toes.

- ❖ Treat every pair of notes in appoggiatura shape (falling semitone from strong to weak) as a gesture of tension and release.

- ❖ Enjoy upbeats. Since every movement is a dance, think of the number of upbeats as preparation for the leading foot to land gracefully on the downbeat. Repeated crotchet/quarter note upbeats gracefully bounce off the ground. Never land heavily (for example, Handel's *And the glory of the lord*).

- ❖ Double dotted notes can be a splendid source of energy. Always sing with the accent on the short note, not the following down beat.

- ❖ Dotted quaver/eighth note and semiquaver/sixteenth note. Three options depending on the degree of intensity: if relaxed, sing as a triplet. If dancing, sing as written with accent on the semiquaver/sixteenth note. If dramatic or stately or military, double dot.

- ❖ Baroque melodies in cantatas or oratorio vary from the dramatic, to the simple, to the orchestral.

- ❖ Simple melodies carry the inflection of the folksong and are appealing in their gentle *legato* and word-based shaping. Remember to keep the intensity growing through them, and find the point of release.

- ❖ Dramatic sections should be sung with emphasis on words, chord change and rhythmic shape.

- Orchestral melodies should be light, dancing and shaped according to the overall line. Feel the individual short notes as parts of an ever-larger pattern – four quavers/eighth notes relate to 8, then 16 and so on.

- In Bach in particular a melody often consists of more than one line; some parts high and others low. Separate out the voices within the voice, and sing them with varying intensity.

- Trills normally begin on the upper note. (For more detailed performance practice analysis, please see *Recommended further reading*, page 47.)

Mozart to Mendelssohn

In this period the orchestra has taken pride of place in the dancing, the complexity and the drive of the music. Some pieces are still grounded in the counterpoint of the baroque, and others give simple chordal lines to the choir, often underpinned by very fast and complex orchestral writing.

- Keep the dance to the forefront, even when the choral line seems to be a sequence of slow chords. Energise a slow melody, keeping it lifted with a sense of direction.

- Make use of the energy in the upbeat, and release gently on the next downbeat.

- Use contrasting styles to reflect the mood and the orchestral accompaniment (*legato*, *marcato*, highlighted words, sudden accents).

- Revel in the simple moments, and let them speak for themselves.

The 19th century

Romantic music has moved away from the choir and is firmly orchestrally-based. The grand works of Berlioz, Brahms, Verdi and the delicacy of Fauré stand out. Each is different according to nationality, and for the most part the style is achieved by following the composer's instructions. Here the colour of the singing is a product of the vocal style in each country (see *Language*, page 34).

Music in England since Mendelssohn needs careful handling. Any tendency to drift towards sentimentality can be counteracted by reference to the ideas of earlier centuries to which the music pays homage, i.e. dance, lift and shape.

Expression marks are rampant, and adherence to them affects the drama of the music. Basically, duck, weave, drive and float, but please don't wallow!

The 20th and 21st centuries

The complexities of much 20th century music mean that many choirs steer clear, which is a shame, because there is reward in focused work on difficult pieces, provided that the result is musical and has conviction.

❖ Explore the composition musically and emotionally, and convey its intention to the singers.

❖ Don't let it be a minefield of difficulties, but deconstruct when learning (see *Kick-start your choir*), so that the learning of each element can be a success.

❖ Tackle small sections at a time, and don't necessarily start at the beginning.

❖ Make games of specific difficulties and tackle them in isolation.

❖ Delay putting the music together until the parts are singable by the choristers. A little frustration among the choir can lead to a tremendous moment of revelation when it all comes together.

❖ The character of the music depends very much on the nationality, and can be reached very directly through the colours achieved by the voice (see *Language*, page 34).

Popular cultures and World Music

Popular song of the 20th century can be sung using the vocal production applicable to all singing, with appropriate language and accents. For example, Gospel music is sung in a wide variety of styles, from the simple spiritual to the most exciting belted sound with movement.

Pop songs often use what is now called 'belting' technique, which, contrary to some current concerns, need not be dangerous for the voice. In fact just as the onset of sound is exactly the same as the natural calls of animals and birds, so the 'belted sound' relates back to the cries of babies, and can be heard in street calls worldwide and in the folk songs of Italy. It is the basic sound of songs from Eastern Europe and of African chant. As with all styles the crucial factor is to avoid abuse of the voice. Breathe naturally and don't constrict the airflow or larynx, and all will be well.

8 Language

The musical style of different cultures depends very much on the inflections and vocal colours of the language, coupled with traditions of performing. 'Authentic' performances of music of the past aim to recreate a way of performing not only musical phrases but also idiomatic pronunciation. If we want to speak another language, there is no substitute for talking to a native speaker; no list of hints can replace the real thing. What follows is not a comprehensive guide and cannot replace the real experience of a culture, or a course of study. However, it does offer shorthand ways to get a feel for singing in some different languages and styles, which work in choral singing. Most importantly, native English speakers should try not to think of English sounds when assembling words in another language. Instead, work from the ground upwards and aim for the natural sound colours described below.

Italian

❖ The exercises on starting a vowel in *Mike Brewer's Warm-ups!* originate from Italian singing. The sound begins cleanly, without glottal noise and without 'h'. This can be called 'Mixed onset'.

Italian consonants don't get in the way ...

❖ Italian is a language based on vowels. The seven vowels are: a ('at'), ɛ ('egg'), e ('eh'), i ('ee'), ɔ ('odd'), u ('oo').

❖ Italian consonants don't get in the way. Keep the mouth shape for the vowel, and consonants will work easily.

— 'c' is pronounced as the English 'ch'.

— 'gh' is 'g' as in 'go'.

- 'gi' is ʒ ('zhi'). 'g' before 'a', 'o' or 'u' is hard.
- 'ti' is 'tsi'.
- 't' before other vowels uses the tip of the tongue only and flicks against the top teeth, like a 'd' not vocalised. (Compare with the German and English bright 't' sound behind the teeth, just at the ridge of the gums.)

Language and style

Italy is known primarily for its opera, and so choruses are full of the drama of action. Bright vowels will make the sound carry in a theatre, and a stylistic decision regarding the amount of *vibrato* employed is necessary. Use a fully resonated tone up to the highest notes, except for *pianissimo* passages. In renaissance Italian music a lighter tone, retaining the bright vowels, works well. Aim for rhythmic life and clear articulation, enjoying the dance of each vocal line. (See also 'Latin', page 42.)

German

- ❖ Often used by English choirs in fast passages, the soft German attack has a bit of 'h' in it, but ideally hardly audible and very short. The start of the vowel comes 'on the beat'.
- ❖ German tends to be sung with a rich tone produced by rounding the lips to make an 'o' shape.
- ❖ Despite the profusion of consonant clusters, it is still essential that the vowel starts on the beat, just as in Italian.
- ❖ Unlike Italian, the sung language is modified from the spoken language. The vowels resonate richly, helped by the rounding process.
- ❖ At the same time the depth of tone is reinforced by a slight yawn in the jaw, which lowers the larynx. (It is hard to sing loudly in this position, because of the lack of high harmonics, so make sure you *crescendo* with lots of breath support and sideways expansion in the body. Slightly widen the elbows to help this sensation, rather than trying to force the tone forward.)
- ❖ Like Italian, German has unvarying vowel sounds, so once you have them in mind, they can be applied to every situation.

❖ The sounds 'ü' and 'ö' are a small minefield for English singers, because sometimes they are short ('füllen', 'zwölf'), and sometimes long ('fühlen', 'schön'). However, the basic sounds can be achieved relatively easily:

— On one pitch sing u ('oo') with lips forward. Change the vowel slowly to y ('ü') by gradually raising the front of the tongue. Keep the focus of the sound in the lips, and by gradually moving lips and tongue just a fraction you can feel the subtle changes in vowel. You may even sense or hear the harmonics!

— The sound ø ('ö') can be achieved in various ways once you have found y ('ü'). Singers love to talk about a 'forward' sound, and you can demonstrate this in action as follows:

Find y ('ü') again. Keep singing and open the lips a fraction, taking the tongue a millimetre back and opening the jaw about the same amount. It is likely that an English person trying this will make a bit of an 'er' sound. Try again, this time giving yourself more air by pulling in the stomach a little. You might feel more resonance in the face this time. Try a third time, and now put a thumb and a second finger each side of your nose, just at the edge of the bone. Can you feel some vibration? If you succeed at this you are ready for most German sounds! Quickly check an a ('ah') with face resonance, then ɔ ('o').

— Diphthongs don't happen, except when there are two vowels! The common diphthong 'ei' is pronounced ɑi ('eye', with a long 'aa' and a short 'i' at the end). Try it. 'eu' is pronounced ɔi ('o-y').

— The most difficult German vowel is found in the harmless-looking masculine definite article: 'der', 'den' and 'dem'. It is helpful for English speakers to exaggerate the German vowels: 'der' = der, 'dem' and 'den' can even be pronounced dim and din. The 'en' at the end of a word is hardly sung – think of 'n', or a very gentle ən 'un' (see above).

Just by keeping aware of the forward resonance brought about by rounded lips and lifted tongue, German vowels start to fall into place. If you lose the sensation you will be back to an English accent! You can try these vowel games in a whisper as well as out loud. Feel the changes in the resonance and even the actual pitch of the vowel.

— Vocalised consonants 'b', 'd', 'g' become 'p', 't', 'k' at the end of a word.

— 'v' = 'f'. 'w' = 'v'. 's' at the beginning = 'z'. 'r' is strong and rolled. 'l' is long and resonant.

Language and style

The sound of German varies for different centuries. The most 'Germanic' tone can be found in the 19th century, from Beethoven through Schubert and Schumann to Brahms, Bruckner and Wolf. Look for:

❖ Lyrical line at the centre of performance.

❖ A feeling of long phrases, even when verse lines are short.

❖ Long vowels combined with clarity of diction – the combination of continuous sound-making in the vowel with lip and tongue movements bringing the rhythm to life.

❖ A joy in harmony and chord change, with flexibility in pulse to accommodate 'moments' in the music.

❖ Whispering ***pp*** tone with slight 'h' attack.

❖ In earlier music – 18th century and before, national barriers were much less clear, and Italian influence in Germany is evident in musical style and thus in sound. (See 'Latin', page 42.) For example the music of Schütz and his contemporaries benefits from a bright tone and light, short, rhythmical phrasing, concentrating on internal rhythms in each voice.

French

❖ Onset tends to be soft and caressing, and can be slightly breathy in some styles.

❖ English people generally find the French language hard to imitate because of what we English call its 'nasality'. The tongue tends to be held high, the soft palate low and the pharynx narrow.

Experiment 1

Sing a ('ah') on one lowish pitch, with raised soft palate and resonating cheekbones. Close the nose with two fingers and feel the sound continue. Put a hand over the mouth and feel the sound stop. Hum 'hmmm' down the nose.

(Hand over mouth, sound goes on; hand over nose, sound stops). 'Hmmm' down the nose with the mouth covered, and change to ɑ ('ah'). Take a hand from the mouth, pulling in the stomach slightly to give a little extra air, and enjoy the nasal sound. Try all the vowels in this way. There are plenty of open vowels in French speech, but by concentrating on the nasal sound in rehearsal, a consistent French sound is created (rather than 'translating' each vowel from English).

I find it helps with French

The French language is hard to imitate because of what we call its 'nasality'

Experiment 2

Sing on one tone or up a scale 'je suis dans le jardin'. How did you score? (Perfect French speakers keep reading, because you may have to teach others!) Test each vowel – 'je', sing 3ø ('zhoe'). Now put a hand over the mouth, which makes the sound totally change. Keep the new sound and take your hand away (adding some extra air from your support) – this is close to French. Sing 'swi'. Put a hand over the mouth, trying to keep the sound and feeling it in the nose. Take the hand away, add more air and let the tongue remain very high. Sing 'do' (as in 'dog'). Put a hand over the mouth, and let the sound find its way into the nose. Take the hand away with added air support and keep lips and tongue as they are. Repeat with 'le' ('lur'), 'jar' ('zhaa'), rolled 'rr' (might take some practise). 'din' ('da' – nasal). Keep the smiling face, raised tongue and the sense of the high harmonics in the nose and you are halfway to singing in French. Now a subtle bit, as the word 'suis' has an exciting diphthong. In French the 'u' is pronounced as the German y ('ü'). Sing 'sy' ('sue' – Girl's name with Glaswegian accent). Now assemble 's-y-i', whispered. Join up, and sing. In singing, as in speech, the second vowel is held and accented.

Consonants are much the same as in speech; dramatic and with lots of lip movement. Repeat the experiment above, focusing this time on the consonants. Remember:

— 'j' = ʒ ('zh')

— 'gn' = ɲ (as in 'onion')

— 'u' = German y ('ü')

— 'en' = ɔ ('o' in nose as above)

— 'in' = a ('aa' in nose)

— 'eu' = ø ('ö' in German as above)

Language and style

❖ Breathing is a little shallow (as in everyday speech), so French is an ideal language for gentle, intimate performance (for example, Ravel, cabaret, Duruflé or Poulenc songs).

❖ Because the resonance is nasal, the high harmonics make the sound bright and light. The nasal vowels thus have their own singing quality.

❖ French performers emphasize expression through the words rather than aiming for consistency of singing tone. However, the dynamic range is smaller than in most languages, and dramatic effects come from articulation of consonants, accents and sudden dynamic changes.

❖ Top notes are generally 'floated' since the strong support needed for full voice is not appropriate.

❖ Take any popular French song, and look at the phrase lengths. They are almost always one or two bars/measures long. Refer to Duruflé or Poulenc, or back to Debussy songs. Each phrase is worth one shrug of the shoulders, or, if you like, one shallow breath.

❖ The musical rhythms are dictated by speech, so plainsong or chant is a natural extension. Try speaking the text of your song first, then sing it with the verbal stresses you have spoken. It makes the quavers/eighth notes uneven, not only in intensity, but also in length – lengthen the important syllables and lighten and slightly shorten the uninflected ones.

❖ Launch each phrase and then let it drift away from you. Rarely is the last note a strong one. Don't let the phrase end sag, but rather allow it to float upwards into the air (lift the support muscles).

* French music loves to paint impressions, and the singer is a little aloof from sordid reality (Edith Piaf being the remarkable exception). Sing the opening bars/measures of 'Sanctus' from the *Requiem* by Fauré, and then by any other composer.

English

* Onset varies for different styles and effects, so practise the mixed onset of Italian.
* Some popular contemporary styles use a harder approach in which you can feel the glottis click – the 'cry' of country and western music, for example.
* Fast passages in Baroque music can benefit from a slight aspiration.
* Having at least 15 vowels means there is a bigger palate of sound colours, although most English speakers distort the vowels with closed mouth and constricted throat, which has the effect of making many vowels sound the same. (Test this by listening carefully to a televised interview.)

♪ T'was in the summer of 2004, That I moved down from Putney to Padstow......

* English is littered with diphthongs and tripthongs, adding to the difficulty of creating a pure vowel sound. Scottish and Irish ballads, Cornish folk songs and sea shanties have their own style and flavour, raising the interesting question as to whether to imitate those

Cornish folk songs and sea shanties have their own style and flavour

sounds or find a 'correct' English in which to sing. In the end the particular circumstances will dictate which feels more appropriate. The shorthand way to solve this problem is to use the voice production and the vowels of Italian, modified as needed.

Most dialects miss out consonants regularly, replacing them with glottal stops. We also hate the 'ng' sound (i.e. the back of tongue and soft palate resonance at the end of words like 'ring' and 'song'). It is therefore vital that choirs regularly practise these, and incorporate them in an exaggerated way into rehearsals. So:

* Breathe as in warm-ups, and feel a natural support for the sound.
* Enjoy resonance, and apply sound-making skills from other languages, especially Italian.
* Be inappropriate in the early stages of learning, i.e. parody an operatic version, or a jazz style (this helps with learning the notes, too).
* Sing very clear Italian vowels, lengthening each one and moving very swiftly between syllables.
* Emphasise resonant consonants, giving them extra length to feel the support (often missed out by English people in speech – for example 'l', 'nng', 'mm' and 'nn').
* Attack the diphthongs! Lengthen the important vowel to almost the whole note and slide or flick through the other one ('Yorkshire Italian'). For example: 'rejoice' = 're-jo---iss'. 'Greatly' = not 'gray-tlee' but 'greh--(long vowel on ɛ 'egg') tli'.
* With 'joined-up' words, for example 'Downin', try a 'glottal start' for 'in' – thus 'down. in'. Before starting the word 'in', the vocal folds are closed (glottal stop) and reopened as a new attack on the vowel.
* 'The' can open out to ə as in 'thur' ('thuh') and will then lead to the strong beat that follows.
* 'And' needs to be felt in the hard palate to resonate. Think of south Wales ('ahnd').

Language and style

Since the English language does not naturally sing (except for particular dialects mentioned above), we need to look at the context of a piece of music to create the appropriate singing sounds. For example, to sing an Afro-American spiritual in a business-like English accent simply sounds wrong. We can assimilate the longer vowels of American English by imitation, as we do the slurring of pitch of the blues, the yodel of the cowboy song and the catch in the voice of much 'pop' music. But the secret is to start with the basic breathing, face shapes and vocal shaping of Italian, which we can then adapt to fit English differences.

Latin

The most common language of Christian music, reflavoured by every country and in every century. We have at least two options: Sing it in a way that puts it in its native country of Italy, guessing how it might have been spoken from how Italians speak now; or working out how the composer might have spoken it, according to nationality and century. 'Church Latin' has evolved over a long period, and is loosely based on Italian sounds. This is a good standby for British performances. If you intend to find an authentic pronunciation for a particular period or nationality then life is harder, but can be rewarding.

- ❖ Use Italian vowels and all will be simple, but check that 'ae' is ε ('eh' as in 'egg').
- ❖ In most cases, use Italian pronunciation for consonants.
- ❖ For English Renaissance: 'c' = 's', 't' = 't', 'gi' and 'ge' = ʒi ('zhi') and ʒε ('zhe'). Also vowels can be more like English, especially in names ('Israel' or 'Jesus' for example).
- ❖ For German music: 'qu' = 'qv' (for example 'qvi tollis'). Vowels are more covered: 'o' changes from ɔ ('dog') to o ('born'), ε ('eh') becomes ə ('uh'), 'Amen' becomes ɑmən ('Amuhn'). 'i' becomes y ('ue'), 'c' becomes 'ts'.
- ❖ German Latin pronunciation works well for 19th and 20th century music, whereas in the Renaissance Germans tended to use Italianate pronunciation. Bach can be sung in both ways.
- ❖ Eastern European languages tend to agree with German sounds, but consult a native speaker if you want 'authentic' Latin. (See also *Recommended further reading*, page 47.)

Troubleshooting Latin

- ❖ The intrusive 'r', for example 'Gloriarin', 'Hosannarin': Stop the sound gently between the words (glottal stop) – thus 'Gloria. in', 'Hosanna. in' ('Hosanine' works beautifully if *legato*).

- Consonant group in 'Excelsis': I recommend Italian ('ex-chelsis') pronunciation here, but in English Renaissance music you can lose some consonant sound by singing 'ekchelsis', or the cathedral compromise 'eggshallsis', or even 'eksellsis'. These have the advantage of shortening the disturbance in sound caused by the stream of consonants.

- Soft 'g' sound before some vowels ('e' and 'i'): normally the sound is as in 'j', but in Renaissance English music it can be softened further to ʒ ('zhe'), so 'in rege' becomes 'in reje' or even 'in rezhe'.

- With the intrusive diphthong, for example in 'Kyrie', sing 'ki-ri-eh' ('egg') not 'Ki-ri-ei'.

- As with Italian, use the vowels to carry the music.

- Take care over excessive consonants: 'Kyrie' needs only a gentle stroke on the 'k'. The soft 's' (as in 'sanctus') is also a valuable asset. Keep the sound short and take it from the onset. Practise making tiny repeated 's' sounds, maybe pointing a finger gently with each one. Feel the body support and gentle lift.

Russian

- A clean Italian onset is usual, with slow resonant consonants where applicable. Note that the larynx is held lower than in Western European languages, which reduces the high harmonics and enhances the lower ones.

- Open vowels are Italian with a slightly darker colour.

- Closed or covered vowels are richer and rounder.

- Resonant consonants are much longer than in English ('v', 'z', 'm', 'n' and especially 'zhe').

- Vocalised plosives (e.g. 'b', 'd', 'g') are heavier.

Language and style

Much Russian church music is slow, and it is effective to delay downbeats with long consonants. Take care not to overdo this and produce a parody. There is more emphasis on the bass part than in Western church music. The basses are seen as a separate element in the vocal orchestration, and there are sections with no bass part to provide contrast. The tenor has great importance, deriving from plainsong, and care is needed in balancing upper parts. A good strategy is to ask some sopranos to sing alto, and indeed if you are short of tenors, add some low altos if appropriate. Pay special attention to the need for sopranos above the upper pasaggio (E top space and upwards) to darken the vowels.

African and Pacific Languages

The sounds of African and South Pacific languages are similar to Italian, but tend to be weighted with strong, physical support. Keep vowels simple, and enrich them with resonance. Most music is rooted is movement.

Space does not permit mention of the music in many languages now available through publication and the internet. Direct contact with native speakers is crucial and strongly recommended. Or better still, invite a guest conductor from that country.

❖ After all the rehearsal, make sure that all is in place for a relaxed and concentrated experience of the music.

❖ The conscious brain is always worrying about the here and now: 'Am I getting it wrong?', 'Can I face this audience?', 'Can I get through this high passage?', 'Can I survive this evening?', 'Will they like it?', 'How I hate this music', 'Why did I come?', 'Where is the British Consul?' etc. Forget yourself.

❖ Be aware of the two halves or your brain when conducting, and like an actor, involve yourself totally in the emotion of the music. At the same time, stand back and observe yourself doing it – not to assess yourself or worry about things that are wrong, but to monitor how the ship is sailing, and tweak the controls as needed.

❖ Be sure about your intentions, leading your singers through the musical trails and paths. Be convinced yourself in order to inspire conviction in them.

❖ Communicate confidence, not panic (hard for all of us, but think positive, and positively take time to relax).

Honestly! I could do better than THAT!

Stand back and observe yourself doing it ...

❖ Dominate the hall in which you are performing. Test the acoustic early on in the final rehearsal, and let the singers enjoy the sound that comes back to them. Reinforce this in the concert. Let final notes finish, then keep the frame of silence. The conductor has control until the arms fall and release it.

❖ There is no need to 'project' the sound out to the audience. Resonance in the body makes for much more resonance in the room or hall (see resonance games in *Mike Brewer's Warm-ups!*).

❖ Bring the audience to the sound (not the other way around!).

❖ Use *pianissimo* and silence as a positive force.

❖ Don't rehearse up to the last minute, as anything learned then will not be remembered. People always revert to previously learned behaviour when under pressure (see 'The five times rule', page 8).

❖ Ensure that singers have different memories of each experience, for example: visual, from your gesture; aural, from the repeated sounds and blend from rehearsals; emotional, from the degree of intensity of each section; mental, in being aware of the notes, how to sing them and the purpose and function of the music; kinaesthetic, from the muscular memory of how each note fits (see *Memory*, page 8).

❖ Ensure that the choir knows what you want, and is ready to respond to your signals, which should be clear and confident. Remember that lifting your hands doesn't mean the sound will stop.

❖ Keep the creative element. Give them the unexpected and ride on the adrenalin.

❖ Ensure that your singers are focused on the music rather than themselves. The audience will not notice mistakes, but they will notice insecurity very quickly.

❖ Always communicate with facial expression, however subtle. Avoid the negative body language of singing only into the copy.

❖ If really nervous, assume another character: either a more happy and confident version of yourself, or a character involved in the music itself.

❖ Above all, enable performers and audience to feel better than they did before.

Recommended further reading

Appelman, D. Richard: *The Science of Vocal Pedagogy*, Indiana University Press

Brewer, Mike: *Mike Brewer's Warm-ups!*, Faber Music

Brewer, Mike: *Kick-start your choir*, Faber Music

British Voice Association: *Voice Care and Development for Teachers*, British Voice Association

Copeman, Harold: *Singing in Latin* (Oxford)

Corp, Ronald: *The Choral Singer's Companion* (Thames/Elkin)

Ehret, Walter: *The Choral Conductor's handbook*, Boosey and Hawkes

Harris, Paul & Brewer, Mike: *Improve your sight-singing*, Faber Music

Hill, David: *Giving Voice*, Kevin Mayhew

Jones, Kate: *Keeping your nerve!*, Faber Music

Miller, Richard: *The Structure of Singing*, Schirmer

Miller, Richard: *English, French, German and Italian Techniques of Singing*, The Scarecrow Press. Inc.

Milne, A.A.: *Winnie the Pooh*, Dean

Sundberg, Johann: *The Science of the Singing Voice*, Northern Illinois University Press

Telfer, Nancy: *Successful Warmups*, Neil A. Kyos Music Company

Ternstroem, Sten: *Acoustics for Choir and Orchestra*, Royal Swedish Academy of Music

Van Camp, Leonard: *Choral Warm-ups*, Lawson-Gould

Woodgate, Leslie: *The Choral Conductor*, Ascherberg, Hopwood and Crew

Acknowledgements

This book is the result of practical experience; the contents summarise ideas that have worked with choirs of many different types. Each new workshop or rehearsal creates fresh opportunities to solve problems and seek new images, as no idea comes from a fixed starting point. As ever I offer thanks to my colleagues Deb, Jebbie, Felicity, Tim and Greg from the National Youth Choir for endless support, inspiration and kind advice, and to the NYC students for many hours of indulgent experiment with sound. The National Youth Chamber Choir, *Laudibus* has also focused on every aspect contained in this book.

Thanks to James Demster for valuable suggestions on IPA and making sense to American readers, and in offering his own wealth of experience in vocal techniques. Much of the content has been road-tested in detail by: James's professional choir in Mexico City, the *Madrigalistas*; 15 choirs in the states of Mexico, kindly arranged by Ana-Patricia Carbajal and Victor Gonzales; 24 different choirs in Singapore, inspired by Nelson Kwei; and the wonderful girls' choir *Cantamus* in England, whose conductor Pamela Cook has been a source of inspiration to me for many years. Special thanks to my editor, Leigh Rumsey, who combines a rare vision for an overall project with a ruthless dedication to detail, all of which she achieves with endless patience and charm. Thanks also to Sandra for positively critical proofreading, Lin Marsh for her advice on popular musical styles, and to Kathryn Oswald and Richard King for making this book happen.